My First Ta
With
God!
Written by: Makesha Williamson
Illustrated by: Lireal Mitchell & Michaela Licorish

ACKNOWLEDGEMENTS

To my grandmothers,
Roberta Robinson and Mary Lee Tutt-Smith.

To my amazing mother, Regina Tutt-Williamson-Welch.

To my beautiful daughters, Tiffany Williamson & Crystal Timothy, and my granddaughters, Imani Rowell, Amaria Williamson, & An'Dreyah Williamson.

To my sisters for life:
Charnissa McKnight, Lakeisha Bradley-Eaddy,
Nakima Gorkin-Williams, Shanita "Tonya" McKnight, Jameika Cooper, Michelle Gibson,
Natanya Russell, Keisha Wilson, Sakina Mckintosh & Adrienne Imani

A special Thank You to my friend and sister for life, the most talented and amazing woman I've ever met, Ms. Joyce Licorish of Dream Empire Publishing!

To Minister Buquilla Ervin-Cannon my #1 supporter.
To the late Mrs. Louise Rembrent-Rice, who was the very first person to invest in me and my dreams.
To the late Mrs. Maxann Crotts-Harvey, who always encouraged me to never give up!

Paperback: ISBN: 9798321862735
Book Designed & Published by: DreamEmpire Publishing
www.DreamEmpirePublishing.com | info@dreamempirepublishing.com
(678)539-0997

DEDICATION

This book is dedicated to my
Grandmother Roberta Robinson.

Thank you for teaching me how to pray and trust GOD!

Additionally, I want to thank all my family and friends for their unconditional support and everyone who supported me over the years, you are so appreciated.

My name is Kesha and I am excited about talking to GOD for the first time.

I have watched my grandmother
talk to GOD many times.

Last Sunday I asked her,
"Excuse me Grandma,
who are you
talking to?"

Grandma said,
“Shhhh! I’m talking to GOD!”

I waited for my grandma to finish talking to GOD.

Later that day, Grandma said,
"Kesha, baby, when you see someone talking to GOD, you don't interrupt them. It's rude. Okay, baby?"
"Yes Ma'am, I'm sorry.
Will you teach me how to talk to GOD?"

I smiled when Grandma said,
"Yes, baby, I would love to.
You can come and spend the
day with me next Sunday, and
we will go to church in the
morning.
After church, we will eat
Sunday dinner, and just before
we go to bed, I will teach you
how to talk to GOD."

I was so excited, the entire week!
I couldn't wait until Sunday!

I daydreamed what I would say to GOD
while I was at school.

I practiced what I would say to GOD
while I was on the playground.

Finally, the day arrived, it was Sunday and I was so excited, I could hardly wait to get inside.

The sun was out and the day was beautiful. So was grandma in her pretty white dress.

After service, grandma told me to change into my play clothes while she got dinner ready.

I was so excited because I knew it was almost time!

After Sunday dinner, I couldn't
wait to get ready for bed!
Grandma noticed and asked,
"Now Kesha, why are you in
such a rush?"
"I'm ready to learn how to
talk to GOD Grandma."

Grandma laughed, and hugged me.

After taking a bath and brushing my teeth, Grandma called me to my bedroom .

"Kesha baby come on.
You were so excited to learn how to talk to GOD that you rushed me all day, now you're taking forever!" Grandma said, laughing. "Are you ready now?"
"Yes Grandma, I'm Ready!"

"Okay baby go to the side of
the bed, get on your knees, and place
your hands together."

"Now, close your eyes," Grandma said.
I closed my eyes and tried to imagine GOD, but couldn't see anything.
"Grandma I can't see you, I can't see anything!"
Grandma replied, "That's okay baby, you don't need to see me. When you are talking to GOD, you are supposed to give Him your full attention."
"Okay Grandma."

Grandma kneeled beside me and said, "Repeat after me ..."

Grandma said,
Now I lay me down to sleep,
I pray the Lord my soul to keep.
If I should die before I wake.
I pray the Lord my soul to take.

And I repeated ...
Now I lay me down to sleep,
I pray the Lord my soul to keep.
If I should die before I wake.
I pray the Lord my soul to take.

And together we said,
Amen.

“Is that all I say to GOD, Grandma?”

Grandma said, “Well, that’s where you start. You can ask GOD to protect you, your mom & dad, and your brother. You can tell GOD how your day went and ask for advice. And to listen, you just have to pay attention to everything you want answers to.

"You can tell GOD anything and everything you want and ask Him to help you with things big and small. You can trust that He hears your prayers. That, my beautiful granddaughter, is called praying and having faith."

"Wow, just imagine all the things I could talk to GOD about.
But, Grandma, do I talk to GOD only on Sundays?"

Grandma replied, "No ma'am, you can talk to GOD every single day.
As many times as you want!"

"Good, now you try on your own,
and when you finish your
prayers, it's time to go to bed."

So, I kneeled and closed my eyes as I prayed on my own, for the very first time.

"Hi GOD, it's me Kesha, please keep my mommy, my daddy, my brother and my cousins safe. But most of all GOD, please keep my grandma safe because I need her to teach me more about you."

"Good, now say Amen."

AMEN.

The End.

Made in the USA
Columbia, SC
09 August 2024